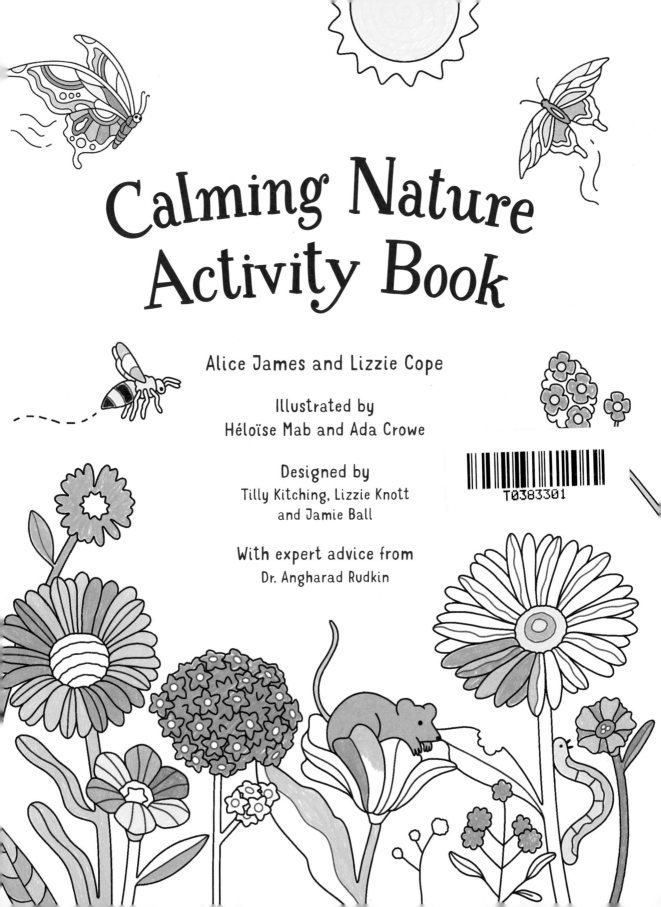

Calming Nature
Activity Book

Alice James and Lizzie Cope

Illustrated by
Héloïse Mab and Ada Crowe

Designed by
Tilly Kitching, Lizzie Knott
and Jamie Ball

With expert advice from
Dr. Angharad Rudkin

T0383301

Spending a little time with nature, from indoor houseplants to wilderness adventures, is GREAT for your body and brain. This book is all about getting stuck into nature, and feeling its wonderful, calming effects.

You can find nature...

...in parks

...in a garden or yard

...on a balcony

Brain scientists called psychologists think that spending time in nature can make you calmer and more positive. It's known as green therapy.

...and in the countryside.

You don't need to do the activities in order – just dip in and out and enjoy relaxing with nature.

There are activities in this book for all of these places, as well as lots you can do at home.

Look out for this symbol. If you scan it with the camera on a smartphone or tablet, it will take you to a piece of calming music or nature sounds.

USBORNE QUICKLINKS

For links to the music and nature sounds chosen for this book and to websites with even more activities, visit usborne.com/Quicklinks and type in the title of this book.

Please follow the internet safety guidelines at Usborne Quicklinks.
Children should be supervised online.

Head out on a nature hunt. Can you track down one of each of these types of things? There are some hints to help you out. When you spot something, write down what you found, and hunt for the next one.

Fallen leaf

Daffodil

Something yellow

Dandelion

Bark

Pine cone

Something rough

Thorn

Seed case

Something spiky

Shell

Nettle

Pebble

Chestnut seed

Something smooth

Driftwood

You don't need to touch or pick up any of these things – just look for them and note them down when you've found them.

Something green

Caterpillar

Leaf

Spongy
moss

Rose

Something you can smell

Rocks

Something heavy

The sea

Cut grass

Log

Butterfly

Something light

A reflection

Maple or
sycamore seed

Feather

Doodle onto these raindrops
and fill in the clouds.

Scan this QR code to listen to peaceful sounds of falling rain while you draw.

Psychologists think that the patter of raindrops helps you feel calm, because the sound is constant and predictable. That means your brain can relax and tune out everything else.

Drawing things when you're outdoors can be a great way to slooooooow down and really look at the world around you. Use this space to draw a scene from nature - or focus on just a few things.

Draw what you can see - from big landscapes to little flowers.

Which direction is the light coming from? Press harder with your pencil to add shadows.

If you need more time, you could take a photo. Then keep drawing when you get home. Lots of artists do this.

You can't be outside all the time – but you can keep little pieces of nature inside to enjoy every day.

Keep a houseplant. They're easy to find and come in all sorts of shapes, sizes and varieties.

Peace lily

Begonia

Fern

These plants like being in a bathroom, where the air is moist.

Cacti and succulents like a dry, sunny spot. You hardly have to water them at all.

Psychologists think having plants inside your home can make you feel happier, calmer and more relaxed.

Open up curtains or blinds to let in LOTS of light. Can you hear any nature sounds through your window? Scan this QR code for extra nature sounds to relax with.

Grow herbs in your kitchen. You could start with seeds, or buy a living herb plant.

Parsley

Rosemary

Basil

Herbs can be used in cooking and they'll taste even better knowing you grew them yourself!

Hang up nature art. Even looking at *pictures* of nature can help you feel calmer. Decorate your walls with photos or drawings you love.

Many trees are HUNDREDS of years old.
They've stood growing in the same spot while
people have come and gone around them.
Imagine you are an enormous, ancient tree and
write about what you've seen on the next page.

What has lived in your branches?
How many creatures have you
given a home to?

Are you near the sea, or on
a hill, or in the grounds of
a mighty castle?

Where in the
world are you
growing?

What have
you seen?

Scientists think the
oldest tree in the world
might have been growing
for nearly 5,000 years.

MOVE your body and take BIG BREATHS while you do it, with these stretches inspired by seaside creatures. You can scan this code to listen to the sounds of the sea as you stretch.

Still as a shell

Curl up your legs and sit steady like a shell nestled into sand.

Moving your body gets your heart rate up. When it goes back down, you feel calmer.

Starfish stretch

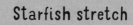

Stretch your arms and legs out WIDE.

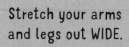

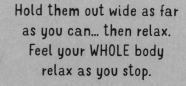

Hold them out wide as far as you can... then relax. Feel your WHOLE body relax as you stop.

One-legged wader

Sea birds called waders often stand on one leg in the sand. They do it to stop themselves from getting too cold on chilly days.

Balance on just one leg. How long can you stay still? Focus your eyes on something that's not moving, as this will help you balance.

Puffer fish breaths

Puffer fish can inflate themselves into round balls, to make themselves too big and difficult to eat.

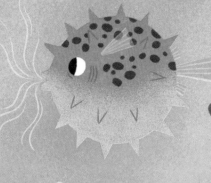

FILL your lungs up with air as you do a BIG breath in.

Feel your chest EXPAND like a puffer fish.

Then let all the air back out.

Whooooosh

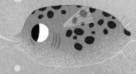

Bring nature right to your doorstep by creating these little safe spaces for wildlife.

Feed the birds

1. Spread peanut butter over the outside of a cardboard tube.

2. Then roll the tube in birdseed.

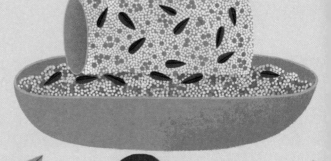

3. Push the tube onto a small branch, or use string to hang it up.

Replace the feeder when it gets old or soggy.

Make a water bath

Fill a wide, shallow bowl with water and add a few stones. Place the bowl in an open area for animals to drink or splash around.

Keep it filled up in hot weather – that's when wildlife needs it the most.

Build a bug home

Turn a small box into a house full of hidey holes for insects to explore.
Starting at the bottom, build up lots of tightly packed layers...

Ridged
cardboard rolled
into tubes

Dry hay or
straw

Pine
cones

Bundles of sticks
tied with string

Pieces of
bamboo cane

Wood
chips

Cardboard tubes
stuffed with dry leaves,
twigs and bark

Put your bug home outside for beetles, ants or other creepy
crawlies to visit. If it rains, move the box under cover to keep it dry.

It's the middle of summer and this meadow is bursting with life. Brighten up all these wildflowers. You could come back to it again and again.

Listen to this soothing music as you work.

A TANKA is a five-line Japanese poem, often inspired by the beauty of nature. Try writing your own tanka following the tips below.

A tanka doesn't have to rhyme, but it has a set number of syllables in each line.

Spring morning

Sunrise glowing gold

Blossom sweetness fills the air

Cool breeze strokes my cheeks

Birds begin to chirp and sing

A bright new day is starting

The first line has five syllables, the second has seven and the third has five.

The final two lines each have seven syllables.

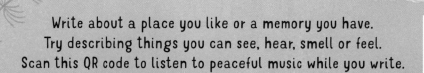

Write about a place you like or a memory you have.
Try describing things you can see, hear, smell or feel.
Scan this QR code to listen to peaceful music while you write.

You could use some of these words to inspire you...

golden sand   long shadows   sparrow chatter

stars twinkle   ripples   moonlight   icicles

crashing waves   crisp leaves   swooping   petals unfurl

Lots of things in the natural world are very small – you might walk past hundreds of tiny creatures every day without even noticing them. Use this simple bug identifier to delve deeper into nature and find out what some of them might be.

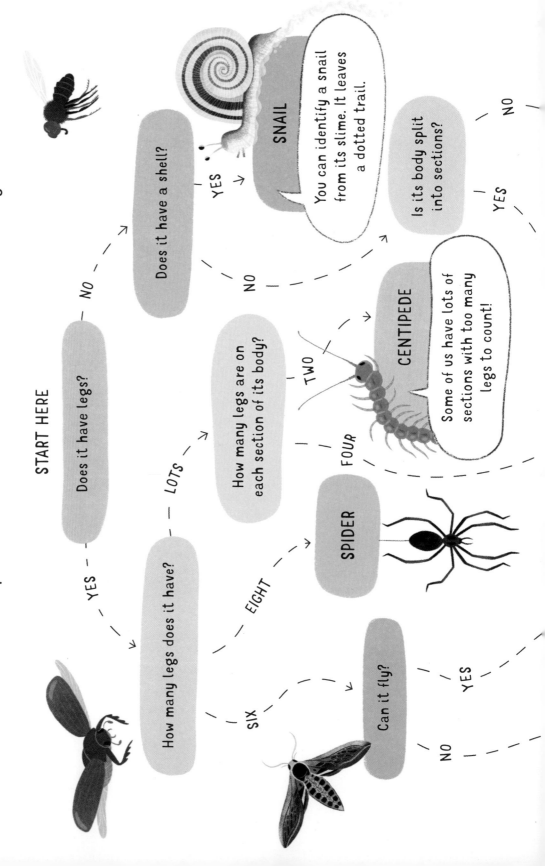

START HERE

Does it have legs?

NO → Does it have a shell?

YES → SNAIL

You can identify a snail from its slime. It leaves a dotted trail.

NO → Is its body split into sections?

NO

YES → CENTIPEDE

Some of us have lots of sections with too many legs to count!

YES → How many legs does it have?

LOTS → How many legs are on each section of its body?

TWO → CENTIPEDE

FOUR

EIGHT → SPIDER

SIX → Can it fly?

NO

YES

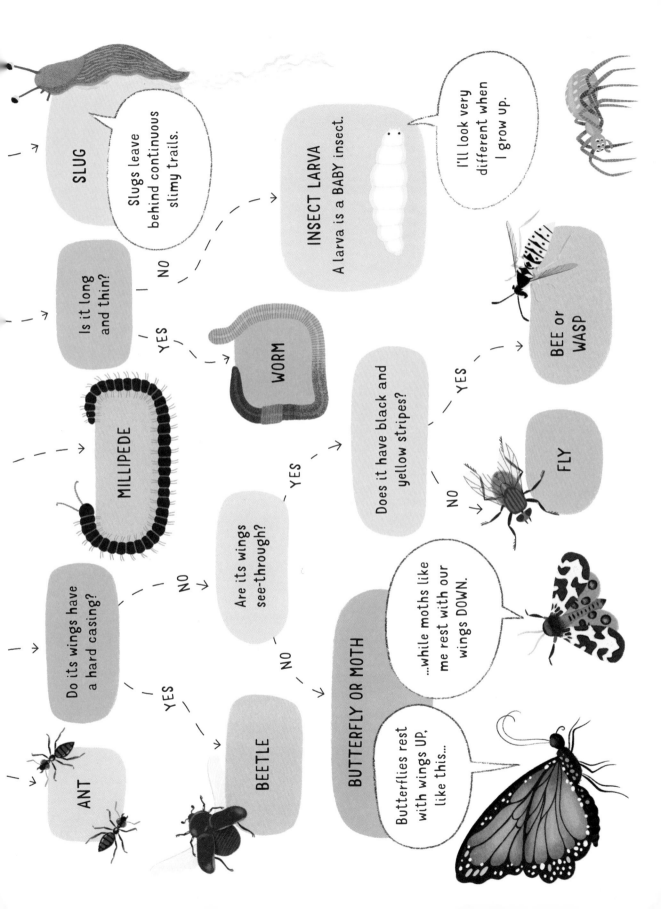

Fill this night sky with dazzling stars,
distant planets and a Moon. Here are some
ideas to create images on black paper.

Use a hole punch on
some scrap paper
and stick in the
little circles that
you cut out.

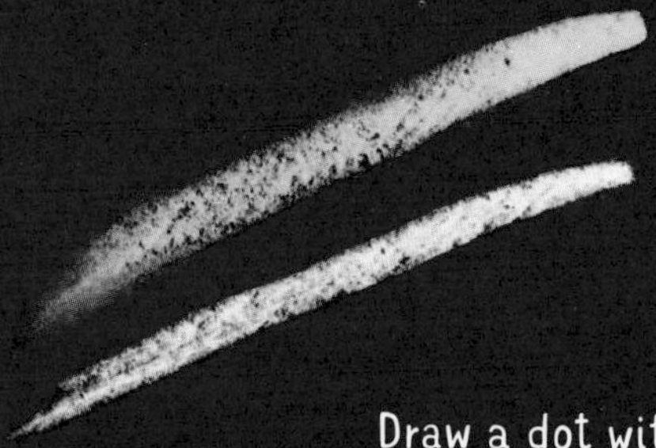

Draw a dot with a chalk, and
smudge it with your finger
to create a shooting star.

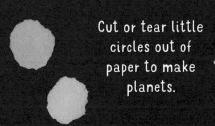

Cut or tear little circles out of paper to make planets.

Draw with a silver pen or white pencil.

Splatter white paint with an old toothbrush.

Listen to starry music while you fill the sky.

Stick in sparkly sequins.

There is so much to know about the AMAZING natural world.
Collect extraordinary facts and add them to this
FACT FOREST as you discover new things.

There's an entire rainforest growing inside the world's largest cave in Vietnam.

On Lake Titicaca in South America, people live on floating islands made of reeds.

The world's oldest tree is nearly 5,000 years old. It's a bristlecone pine known as Methuselah.

Bumblebees can fly higher than the tallest mountain in the world.

Sea otters hold paws while they sleep so they don't drift apart.

Every plant starts off as a teeny seed, which grows into a plant over time. Most plants just need a little bit of soil, a sunny spot and some water. Here are a few plants that are easy to grow at home.

Carrots

You can grow carrots in an old bucket. Push seeds about 2cm (1 inch) into the soil.

Feathery leaves grow on top, while carrots grow under the soil.

Cress

Cress just needs a soggy piece of paper towel on a flat surface or scrunched into eggshells. Scatter seeds, keep them damp, and watch cress grow.

The first cress shoots only take a day to appear, and it's ready to cut after one week. Try putting the shoots in a sandwich.

Avocados

To start growing an avocado plant, put a clean avocado pit in moist paper towel and leave it in a dark place.

When a green shoot appears, place the pit above a jar of water.

Pumpkins

Put one pumpkin seed in each pot in springtime. When the last frost is over, they can be planted outside where they'll grow pumpkins.

Sunflower

You can start sunflowers in an old cardboard tube. They can grow VERY tall, so you'll need to get them a bigger pot.

Tall plants might also need propping up with a stick or cane as they grow.

Sweet peas

You could use old plastic tubs like these yogurt containers, to start your seeds off in. Just make some holes in the bottom for water to drain away. Water them when the soil looks dry.

Doodle patterns and scales on these tropical fish. Add doodles to the coral and rock too, and listen to this underwater music as you go.

Watching the birds near where you live can help you feel connected to nature right on your doorstep. Find a comfy spot outside, or next to a window, then watch and wait...

How many birds can you see?

Notice how they move. Are they swooping, hopping around, or perching in a tree?

A good time to watch birds is around sunrise or sunset, when they're most active.

Can you hear any chirping or singing? Try to pick out different calls.

You could keep watching over the next few days or weeks to see if the same birds come back to visit.

Use this space to write about any birds you spot. Don't worry if you don't know their names – just write a few words to describe each one.

Listen out for any bird calls, or scan this QR code to hear some. Make up words based on how they sound and write them here.

TATATAT

KA KAAA

CHURRR

You can make your own natural paints
from vegetables and spices in your kitchen.
This is a good activity to do outside on a nice day.

Drain the juice from a
jar of beetroot (beets)
to make...

Soft pink

Wear an apron so
the paints don't
stain your clothes.

Stir two heaped teaspoons
of turmeric or curry powder
into a small mug of warm
water. Mix it well into a...

Sunny yellow

Add hot water to a mug of
torn spinach leaves and
mash it with a fork.

Wait for five minutes, then
sieve it into a bowl to make...

Leafy
green

Use a paintbrush to make soothing swirls and swooshes with your new plant paint kit. Wash your brush off between the different paints.

Create mini nature rafts that you can bob and float on a stream, pond or even in a bathtub.

There are several ways to make a base for your raft.

You could tie four sticks together at the corners to make the basic shape.

From here you can add more sticks, or pieces of bark to fill it out.

You could use a flat seed case or a piece of bark as your raft instead.

Or bind lots of sticks together with string running over and under each stick.

When you float your raft, you could imagine any worries bobbing away on them.

Once you have a base you can add a sail to help it float.

An easy way is to push a leaf sail onto an upright stick, and wedge it into the base.

Leaf

Stack of leaves

Feather

Piece of bark

Add a pebble as a passenger, or decorate your raft with any other natural treasures you find.

Over 100 years ago, a writer named Rudyard Kipling wrote imaginary stories, called the *Just So Stories*. These stories described how he thought things in nature came to be - such as how the leopard got its spots. Continue the imagined stories on these pages and get lost in your own tall tales.

HOW DID THE...

thunder get its voice?

BOOOOM

_____

_____

_____

_____

_____

_____

_____

_____

_____

_____

_____

_____

HOW DID THE...

tortoise get its shell?

_____

_____

_____

_____

_____

_____

_____

_____

_____

_____

_____

_____

_____

_____

_____

_____

_____

Fill in the intricate patterns on the wings of these moths and butterflies.

Wings are symmetrical – both sides look the same.

Listen along to this fluttery music as you draw.

Some wings blend in, and help the moth or butterfly to hide...

Painted lady

This butterfly has a different pattern on the top and bottom of its wings.

Brimstone

Some patterns are to show off. Fill these wings with dazzling blues and purples.

Blue morpho

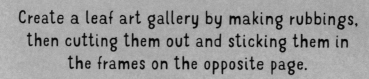

Create a leaf art gallery by making rubbings, then cutting them out and sticking them in the frames on the opposite page.

1. Collect leaves
You can use fresh or dry leaves. Try to find a range of shapes and sizes.

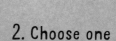

2. Choose one
Select a leaf and place it BOTTOM SIDE UP on a table – the side where you can see the lines on the leaf most clearly.

3. Sketch over the top
Put a thin piece of paper over the top, and rub all over the surface of the leaf with a crayon or pencil.

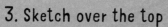

The lines that appear are VEINS. They are little tubes that carry water and nutrients to every part of the growing leaf.

Now cut out your rubbings and stick them in these frames.

Look for leaves with different shapes and textures.

Shade some harder and some softer.

Try using different crayons or pencils.

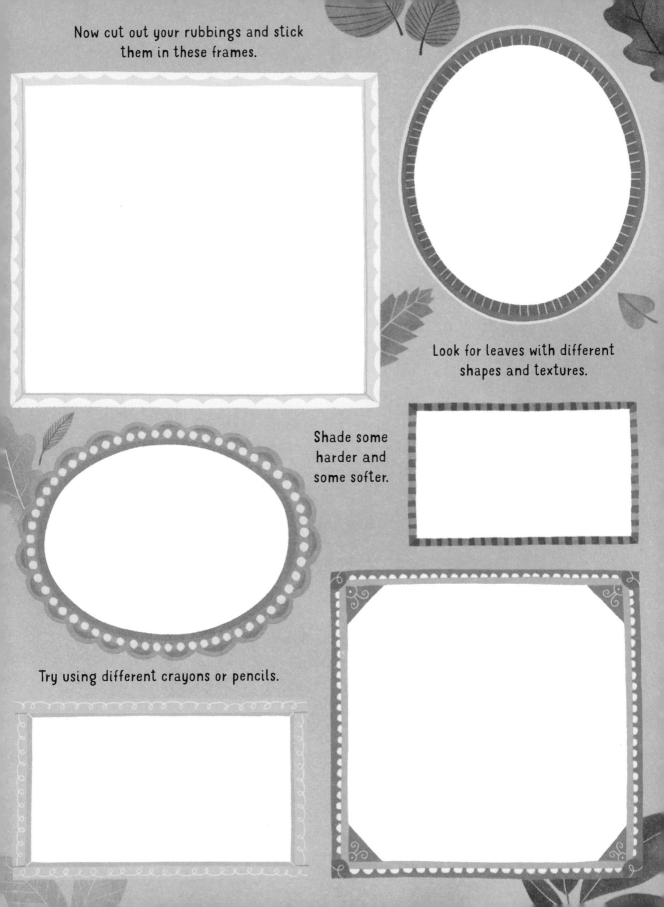

The natural world is full of
millions of types of creatures,
in all shapes and sizes. Use this
space to doodle and draw and
dream up YOUR OWN living things,
with all sorts of different features.

Wings

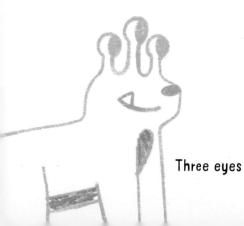

Three eyes

Fur

No legs

Tentacles

Sharp teeth

When you're at the park, in the woods or on a beach,
try your hand at creating a natural work of art.

Draw in the sand

Footprint paths

Use a stick, your finger, or
shuffle your feet to create
BIG ART in the sand.

Stamp some footprints in mud or sand.
Add little stones or gravel to fill the dents,
and leave behind paths of rocky footprints.

Water art

Use a paintbrush dipped in water to draw pictures on the ground or a wall.
It'll dry and disappear, then you can start again.

Stick sculpture

Lay out sticks to form shapes. To make a solid structure you could tie sticks together with string.

Leaf circles

Arrange fallen leaves in decorative circles. You could choose different leaves for different layers of the circle.

Stone faces

Add characters to smooth, dry pebbles with a marker pen.

Wherever you live and whatever time of year it is, the SKY is always there for you to look at and explore. Look up and watch the clouds - which types can you find?

Cirrostratus
A thin, hazy layer high in the sky

Cirrocumulus
Little fluffy blobs - sometimes called mackerel sky

Nimbostratus
A thick, dark blanket

Cumulus
Fluffy white clouds with flat bottoms

Stratus
A low blanket of pale cloud

Cirrus
High, wispy
clouds

Can you see actual clouds now?
Draw or describe them here.

Altocumulus
White, fluffy
blobs

For the most calming
cloudspotting, lie down
on a blanket on a comfy
patch of grass, and look up.
Watch the clouds drift
past, and relax.

Can you help this meerkat find its way through the burrow?

Entrance

Exit

Meerkats spend most of their time in burrows like this one.

The burrow stays the same temperature, however hot or cold it is above ground.

Join the numbers from 1–73 to complete this desert picture. Then fill in the scene with pens or pencils.

Getting lost in puzzles like these can be very relaxing. Just take your time and finish them bit by bit.

Decorate the branches of these woodland trees as they appear at different times of the year.

Use pens or pencils to fill in these fresh spring blossoms.

Summer is here. Doodle lots of leaves onto these branches.

As it gets colder, leaves turn red, orange and yellow. Cut paper from old magazines into leaf shapes and glue them here.

Stick white paper triangles to these wintry branches to make icicles.

Fill in this morning rainforest scene, and listen along to music.

Next time you're out exploring nature, try making a journey stick.
Take some string and find a sturdy stick. As you walk, collect things
you find and tie them to the stick as a record of your travels.
Here are some things you might find...

Feathers

Leaves

Twigs

Moss

Small
pebbles

Fallen leaves

Don't pick any
flowers - leave them
growing for everyone to
enjoy. Once you've finished,
scatter everything back
into nature.

Pine cones

Seeds

You could try making
journey sticks at different
times of year. This is one is
from late summer.

Imagine you're walking along the seashore. What items would you collect along the way? Draw them on this journey stick.

You could use shells, seaweed, pebbles, sea glass and anything else you can find.

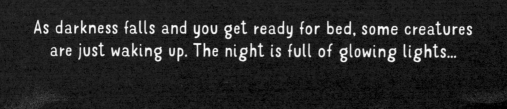

As darkness falls and you get ready for bed, some creatures
are just waking up. The night is full of glowing lights...

Shine a light onto a pale wall and
keep still. Does anything come
and fly into the beam of light?

Moths are
attracted to light.

If you live in the
countryside, you might
be lucky enough to
spot a firefly glowing in
hedges or long grasses.

BUZZ

Turn your light off for a
moment. Stay very still – what
can you hear? You can even do
this through a window.

FLUTTER

SNUFFLE

Some animals use moonlight to guide them in the dark. Is the Moon bright enough to find your way where you are?

Look under a streetlight. Lots of insects buzz around the light – can you hear their tiny wings?

Some nighttime animals have eyes that shine when lights catch them.

A cat's eyes shine yellow.

A fox's eyes shine red.

A frog's eyes shine green.

Use the pictures on these pages as starting points for stories.
Sit back, imagine and write...

What's happening on
these rocky slopes?

_____

_____

_____

_____

_____

What – or who – is this
kingfisher waiting for?

_____

_____

_____

_____

_____

_____

_____

_____

_____

The sun is rising on a
crisp new day. What does
the day have in store?

Fill these pages with leaves you find on your nature adventures.

Find a leaf you like the look of. Always take one from the ground, rather than picking one off a plant.

Flat leaves are easiest, but if your leaf is curled like this, put it flat between two heavy books.

It will dry flat, and you'll be able to stick it in.

ANSWERS

to the desert puzzles

Here's the way
through the maze.

Joining the dots
makes a camel.

Additional illustration by Harry Briggs

Design manager: Stephen Moncrieff

Series editor: Jane Chisholm

First published in 2023 by Usborne Publishing Limited, 83-85 Saffron Hill, London EC1N 8RT, United Kingdom. usborne.com

Copyright © 2023 Usborne Publishing Limited. The name Usborne and the Balloon logo are registered trade marks of Usborne Publishing Limited. All rights reserved. No part of this publication may be reproduced, stored in a retrieval system or transmitted in any form or by any means without prior permission of the publisher. UE. First published in America 2023.

Usborne Publishing is not responsible and does not accept liability for the availability or content of any website other than its own, or for any exposure to harmful, offensive or inaccurate material which may appear on the Web.